Garment Workers of

South Jersey

Garment Workers of South Jersey

Nine Oral Histories

The Stockton Center on Successful Aging
South Jersey Culture & History Center
Kramer Hall

2016

This first edition published 2016 by the Stockton Center on Successful Aging, the South Jersey Culture & History Center, and Kramer Hall.

Stockton University
101 Vera King Farris Drive, Galloway, New Jersey, 08205

Title: Garment Workers of South Jersey: Nine Oral Histories

Copyright © 2016

ISBN-13: 978-0-9888731-8-6

The Stockton Center on Successful Aging (SCOSA) at Stockton University promotes research, education, and services addressing local, regional, and statewide age-related needs and opportunities. SCOSA offers technical assistance, a staff family caregivers support group, training for professionals and students, and funding for faculty research. Older Adult Education Programs are SCOSA's most visible and frequent offerings. In 2015, 2500 participants attended over 200 sessions at sixteen sites throughout Atlantic County and in Manahawkin (Ocean County). Programs are supported by Older Americans Act funding via Atlantic County Government, by Stockton University, and by various SCOSA revenues derived from fees, donations, and sponsorships, advertisements and exhibits at SCOSA's Annual Festival.

The mission of the South Jersey Culture & History Center is to engage both Stockton students and local community members in their own backyards. This volume joins our ongoing offerings of exhibitions, publications, and public programming—all developed by or with Stockton students—and highlighting the rich cultural heritage of New Jersey's eight southernmost counties.

Table of Contents

Preface

An oral history involves the collection and study of historical information using sound recordings of interviews with people who have personal knowledge of past events. While to some "oral history" is a maddeningly imprecise term, we who compiled this book use the term to refer to the method used to collect informal conversations about "the old days of the garment work industry" that occurred in and near the present-day location of Kramer Hall, in Hammonton, New Jersey. From January through May 2015, nine social work students attending Stockton University spent time conducting, recording and editing interviews with actual retired garment workers, their family members, neighbors and coworkers. Magical exchanges of information occurred inside and outside the classroom, as younger students listened to compelling stories told about past times and present experiences; they recorded interviews with people who had a story to tell about a garment industry that existed during a time when unions were just forming and air conditioning was ne'r in existence.

Interviewers used a set of probing questions to elicit stories and data from history-consciousness individuals who were proud of being connected to the South Jersey garment industry of yesteryear. Through these subsequent firsthand accounts of the past, readers can learn about living and working conditions from people who experienced them. Social conditions of the times and workplace are unearthed in each interview snippet and these life histories document the diversity of the American experience and how ordinary people coped with hardships during the late 1930s, early 1940s and beyond. With the assistance of twenty-first-century recording devices and technology the interviewer's note-taking has been enhanced and made more reliable. Our intent is to develop a permanent archival collection of stories about the South Jersey garment industry.

Interestingly, many historians consider oral history as beginning with the work of Allan Nevins at Columbia University in the 1940s. Nevins was the

> . . . first to initiate a systematic and disciplined effort to record on tape, preserve, and make available for future research recollections deemed of historical significance. While working on a biography of President Grover Cleveland, he found that Cleveland's associates left few of the kinds of personal records— letters, diaries, memoirs—that biographers usually rely upon. At this same time the telephone was replacing personal correspondence and Nevins concocted the notion of conducting interviews with participants in recent history to supplement the written record. He conducted his first interview in 1948 with New York civic leader George McAneny, and both the Columbia Oral History Research Office—the largest archival collection of oral history interviews in the world—and the contemporary oral history movement were born."[1]

Whereas earlier interviewing projects focused on the lives of the "elite" who worked in business, politics and society, the scope of oral history widened in the 1960s and 1970s in response to social movements and interest in non-elites. Subsequently and increasingly, interviews have been conducted with blue-collar workers, racial and ethnic minorities, women, labor and political

---

[1] "What Is Oral History?" What Is Oral History? *Visible Knowledge Project.* Accessed April 04, 2016. http://historymatters.gmu.edu/mse/oral/what. html.

activists, and multiple local people whose lives typify a particular social experience. Through the recording of firsthand accounts of many diverse narrators, oral history has helped democratize the historical record.

In summary, "oral history" may be best understood as a disciplined conversation between two people about some aspect of the past considered by them to be of historical significance and intentionally recorded for the record. Although the conversation takes the form of an interview, in which one person—the interviewer—asks questions of someone else—the interviewee or narrator—oral history is, at its heart, a dialogue.

Dr. Lisa E. Cox, Professor
The Stockton Center on Successful Aging
Research Chair and Fellow

Introduction

During World War II, when the clothing factory whistle blew, thousands of women throughout South Jersey responded to the call. They packed their children off to school, made sure all of the ingredients were available for that night's dinner, and then headed out the door.

Factory life was not easy but the women were used to working. Many of them were either Italian immigrants or first-generation Italian-Americans, the wives, sisters and daughters of farmers who tilled the land on small truck farms. Between the late nineteenth and early twentieth century, millions of Italians flocked to the United States, drawn by the promise of a better life for their families. Many of the newcomers chose to move to South Jersey because the open farmland and the forests that reminded them of their homeland. Although living was not always easy, it was better than anything they had known in their native land.

Close-knit, bound together by tradition, the families lived by certain rules: Father was second only to the church as an authority figure. Education was usually considered unnecessary for women since their husbands would provide for them when they married. And, above all, the needs of the family were far more important than the needs of the individual.

As a result, many of the clothing factory workers quit school in their early teen years to help support their families. The additional income that they brought home each week was sometimes just enough to keep the family fed and the mortgage paid.

The "needle trade," as it was known, was considered acceptable work since it mirrored the domestic chores that women performed at home. During the early 1940s, about 6,000 workers in New Jersey annually produced about $38 million in civilian clothing and military uniforms. While most of the regional clothing factories were located in Vineland, others were situated in Atlantic City, Bridgeton, Hammonton, Mays Landing, Landisville and Minotola.

The women earned roughly $15 to $30 for a forty-hour work week but the amount sometimes fluctuated for those who were paid for piece work. The more bodices, collars, cuffs and sleeves they sewed, the more they earned. At the end of the week, that pay envelope was usually turned over to their fathers or husbands without a word of complaint.

But a quiet revolution was brewing—one that did not involve sit-ins or violent demonstrations. It was the revelation that, for the first time, the women were receiving monetary compensation for their work. For many of them, that paycheck was accompanied by a new sense of autonomy and ambition. Although they usually turned it over to the head of the household, they were often rewarded with an allowance that they could save or spend as they saw fit. The clothing factories also brought them a chance to explore the outside world, make new friends, and perhaps even find romance.

Most of these women did not see their decision to work at the local clothing factory as anything that was especially heroic. They never had time for the luxury of self-examination, since they were still often expected to handle all of the household chores at the end of the day, no matter how long their shift had been at the factory.

As a result, while the women themselves may not have considered themselves to be heroes, their stories are worth preserving for a number of reasons. They made major contributions to American industry, and helped develop the unions for the clothing factory workers. But most significantly, while they might not have always achieved their dreams, they pieced together a whole new standard of life for their daughters by demonstrating that any goal could be reached by those who were willing to work for it.

Patricia A. Martinelli, Curator
The Vineland Historical and Antiquarian
Society

Editors' Note

Oral histories are challenging to recreate in written form because they don't always flow in the type of narrative fashion that is familiar to a reader. Often, comments are repeated and trains of thought wander, so it becomes necessary to judiciously edit the "conversation" to allow the most significant points to surface without losing the flavor of the story. In the following accounts, different interviewers used different techniques to elicit information from their subjects, which will be quickly apparent to the reader. Hopefully, we have succeeded in keeping true to the original stories and, as a result, have been able to shed some light on a little-known piece of American history.

Chapter 1

Concetta Bailey

Interviewed by Barbara Edelhauser

My full name is Concetta and they call me Connie. Everybody knew I spent most of my life in what we called a sweatshop, and it was a sweatshop. I am guessing that you already know that that building where Stockton is was a clothing factory. I was born in Philadelphia. I was ten years old when my parents decided to move to Hammonton. My mom used to sing "Do Not Fence Me In."

When I got out of high school, the money was in the clothing factories. I could have gone to a bank or something at that time (but) you had to overinvest in clothes to work with the public. At a shop, you just go (in) regular clothes and you go work.

I started out at seventy-five cents an hour. I started at Bell Sportswear on Second Street. Right now, it is some kind of an office building. I worked there until I had my son. Yeah, I worked a full day, I did put in a lot of overtime, because I was young. When I started there, I was young. I went in as a Miss and came out as a Mother-To-Be. When I started with seventy-five cents an hour, that only reached its peak, and then I automatically went on piecework. And every shop I worked in, I did not work in a lot of shops, but every shop I worked in that is just how it was. I always had to do piecework.

That was making money. When I met my husband, I was making more than him. At Belle Sportswear, the first place I worked, they made ladies skirts. I do not even think they use it now, but at the bottom of the skirt, there was a ribbon binding. That is what I did. I put a ribbon on the bottom of the skirt. That is what I did, by machine. It was just a regular plain machine, with a regular foot on the bottom of it, off it went.

I guess I worked there for five years, then I had my son and stayed home for two years and then I went to one of the biggest shops in town, you probably heard, it was Kessler's. That was Hammonton Park. And I worked there until I got pregnant with my daughter. And there it was pants, they made full suits there; they were the biggest (clothing factory) in town at that time. I guess they had about five hundred people at that time. I am just guessing.

I worked in the coat shop for two years. And at that time it was a piece of, we used to call it bridle. It is like a tape, a white tape. It went on the inside, before they put the lining on the front of the jacket. That is where I stayed for two years. Then I had my daughter and I stayed home. When she was in kindergarten, I went to work at Romolo's on Fairview Avenue. That was men's slacks and I stayed there until the Japanese and Chinese imports started coming in. I stayed there quite a few years. I worked on a big machine there, probably as big as that little hutch (pointing to the corner of her dining room) and maybe double that and it had three little knives. The back pockets of the men's slacks, right here (motioning with her hands), there was a piece I used to put on. It was like a skinny little piece what I would put on and I would cut through the pant leg, with this big machine.

I stayed there until it closed. This was the first time it closed. We were probably, I am guessing, in the middle to late seventies. It closed, and then the Union—Amalgamated Union—called us all back. They were going to reopen it and we did not get no raise and all that crap, just to keep it going. A couple months later, the shop was done. When I worked at Belle Sportswear, they might have had a Ladies Union, that is like sixty or more years ago. I never got any benefit from that.

Let me tell you what I get from Amalgamated Union, a month, for thirty-two years of work, $35.18. Now, if you were a younger person, just starting college that would blow your mind. If I was to get my husband as a death benefit (laughs), it is hysterical. So then, the longest I ever worked would be Romolo's Slacks on Fairview Avenue, where they closed and they reopened and they closed. Then I was home for I do not know how long.

This was all in the late 1970s. And then I get a call one morning. The clothing factories all had foremen and I get a call from this Ralph, who was my foreman when I worked at Romolo's. Since that shop closed, he and another foreman that ran Pianos(?)[1] together thought that the two of them were going to open a little shop, right here off of Third Street. And they collected different operators that they were familiar with. So I went. Still working on the same machine, but then it was a small shop and you had to do whatever job you could do, which was fine. And I lasted there probably about, I do not know, close to ten years and then I decided it was time to change.

I spent a year working down at the casino as a cashier. It was enough. I came back and worked at the bank for ten years and that was it.

Q: How was it working in the factories?

It was just something you did. I never had any problem. It was a job. It was what you call a sweatshop. We never had air conditioning. You know, I used to come home at lunchtime and take a bath and go back five after one, sweating all over again. The thread, the dust, was sticking over here (points to the crease in her elbow). The bottom line of it was, when I went to work for

---

[1] Unclear statement.

Romolo's Slacks on Fairview Avenue, that building was built with air conditioning, but when I started there it was not working and never worked as long as I (was there).

Q: When did your parents come over?

I am Italian born, Italian American. My father was like two years old (when he came from Italy). My mother was born in Philadelphia. Yeah, I have been here forever. I never had a problem working with anybody in (the clothing factories). As a matter of fact, my two best friends who I worked with, we are still best friends. The only thing is, there was always, I do not know, but when you make a working friend there is always a strip of jealousy there because you are out to make a dollar, and (if you do) somebody is not going to make that dollar today.

I never had a problem, but I remember now, what I call these old ladies, which is what I probably am now, as soon as you would start your job, you would hear, "You do not make no money in this place. You can not stay. You gotta go." Well. "How long have you worked here?" "Oh, fifty years." You know what, you are young. You have to learn. But, of course, I never left.

The advantage of the shop work at that time was that, yeah, the shop had seasons. So we stayed with them. We were off a lot, in between collecting unemployment, which was good in its own way. At that time, you did not have to pay taxes on unemployment, but the only thing was, the damper side was, if you got called. You never knew when you were going to get called into work. You know, like maybe the phone did not ring today and then at like 11:30, "You want to come in this afternoon?" Those things did happen, but it all worked. At that time, we were all, "What, we gotta go in this afternoon?"

Q: So, you did not know when you were going to work?

No, it was all according to who was the supplier. We more or less knew. When we went in there like Monday, Tuesday, or Wednesday, we might have just worked a half day for three days and then the boss would say "Well that's about it for a couple weeks now." Or he might say "Next week a big lot is coming in." And that was just the way it was.

And we used to pull tickets off. We were piecework. We used to pull the little tickets of whatever we were working on.

At home, you had to do the cooking, the housework and run with kids for sports and whatever was involved. (The work day was) eight to five, but when we got to Ralph and Eddie's, which were the two bosses that opened the little shop, we would work seven to four. But in the summertime, we all decided we were going to go in like at six for cooler time and get out. And then we took a half-hour lunch. The bosses asked and we said yeah, because it was hot.

So, every piece of garment had a little ticket on it, which had a lot number on it and an amount of each bundle. Everything was called a bundle, tied up. And then we would bring all our tickets home and every Sunday night, I would do homework, with a pencil and paper, and total up how many I did, and then Monday morning you would bring your time sheet in.

Q: Did you buy any of the clothes?

I would guess they were too expensive for me, but I do remember buying two things, maybe one was for me, when we went to Carousel Slacks. I used to like to wear culottes and they were winter culottes and they were winter white, and they must have had a couple extra and asked if anybody wanted to buy them. I think I bought my sister a pair and me a pair. Do not ask me how much they were. I have no idea.

And something interesting at Carousel Slacks, we used to have to call the bank up every Friday to see if our check was good enough to cash, if the money was there. The figure on these checks—what do you think they were, a million? $50, $45, $30. And it was, in its own way, it was nice. That place was the smallest and probably the most comfortable.

We got our vacations. We got our holidays. Yeah, (thanks to) Amalgamated Union, which gave me my big pension of $35.18, we ended up with two weeks (vacation). I was off for the first two weeks of July. And then they gave us one week, Christmas time, which was good. You were home with the kids, Christmas and New Year's. Yeah, and then the holidays, we got normal holidays, but if you did not come in the day before or the day after, you did not get paid. And you did not get paid if you were not working on the job, if you did not punch a time clock. Even though it was piecework, you still had to punch that time clock.

Q: Can you talk about your recent birthday?

I just had a birthday. They gave me a surprise 80th birthday party and it was a surprise. They had it at the bowling alley. It is up the Pike . . . in Hammonton. There is a party room there and they have a restaurant and the irony of the whole thing was that my son lives in North Carolina and my daughter lives in Alaska. But, this all started with, we were going to all go out for a family dinner. Everybody was accounted for, so I knew they were all going to be there that Saturday. (My daughter) insisted that we go to DiDonato's Bowling Alley for appetizers. But the restaurant we were supposed to go to was in Collingswood.

I thought I was going to get a surprise; you see, my sister's boy lives in Massachusetts and they have been having snow right and left there. My sister kept telling me, "I do not know if my son is going to make it, because he has got snow coming off the roof."

My son's oldest boy lives in Atlanta (but) in the back of my mind, I am (thinking) we are going to go to dinner and they are going to surprise me. Josh is going to be there and Tom, my nephew. He did come. My grandson did not come, but my nephew was there and it was a party. They did a good job, considering it was miles away.

Q: How old were you when you had your children?

I should know, let me figure this out. I should know it by heart. Twenty, wait a minute, I was just eighty. My son is, well, it is close, because we were married in September of 1955 and I had my son February of 1957. That would make me like twenty-two, I think. And my daughter was four years later.

Q: Holiday traditions?

Well, when we first made all the dinners? Oh yeah, I made a lot of dinners in (my) house because my sister is ten years younger than me. So she got married like ten years after I did. Well, I am just pulling that out of the hat, you know. And Christmas was here and Thanksgiving was here and maybe even Easter was here. I do not remember, but I remember Christmas and Thanksgiving in this house. And then the kids got big and that was the end of all that. And everybody, the people older than us phased out. My sister built her home and then we split the holidays there. And before you know it, there was nobody there left at the table.

Q: Were special dishes handed down?

You mean to me? Well we kind of worked it through. We never did the seven fishes for Christmas, but we always had something of it. You know, a couple of smelt. Well, you always managed something.

Q: Do you have pictures of anyone you worked with at the garment factories?

I have pictures scattered, that I would have to look for, from the first shop, from Belle Sportswear. But to tell you the truth, I do not even know where they are. They are in a big box with other pictures. A lot of them are old black-and-white ones.

Q: How has Hammonton changed over the years?

Hammonton is a very private town. I do not know what anybody else is telling you, but you have to understand, I am not a Hammontonian, because I was not born here, okay? I love the town, but if you get a real Hammontonian with you, I think different than them. And there is nothing wrong with the thinking.

The population of Hammonton, when I moved (here) when I was a little girl was probably close to what it is today. It is a close-knit town, a lot of people are related and the farmers are the farmers and their ancestors just worked on the farm. We never had a farm—my husband and my father-in-law were like part-time farmers. They had real jobs because they came from the family of sixteen kids. My kids graduated Saint Joe's High School and they went to college and never came back.

Q: Your family were city people?

My father never had a driver's license. It is different. I do not know what you heard, but getting back to Kessler's, this had nothing to do with me but, I do not know if you ever heard that Mr. Kessler, at that time brought in a lot of foreigners. He paid for them to come—a lot of the Greek and a lot of the Italian people, he brought them here, because Kessler's was number one. And a lot of those Italian people are still here, or descendants of them.

Q: Did your family move here because there were a lot of Italians?

I do not know. All I know is we are going to move to Jersey. But the town itself has changed. I would say at one time probably everybody's last name ended in a vowel. Now they end in a vowel, but they are Spanish people, which is all over. Thanks to Hammonton First, the Independent Party that quite a few of us belong to it, they have done a lot with Main Street, Bellevue Avenue. Hammonton is a rich town. You ever come down Central Avenue? All big old homes. A lot of the farmers, they do not (live in town), they live back. You ever take a short cut when you come home through Pleasant Mills Road?

Q: Was Philly compartmentalized by nationality, like a lot of cities were, back then?

The only house I remember was on South Moll Street, which was basically a little bit of all nationalities, but evidently when I was born, Dad lived in a different part of South Philly, where I was. They took me to get baptized and the priest would not baptize me, because we were Italian. That was stupid. Well I started out in South Philly. I always went to Catholic school. Then I ended up over here, at Saint Joe's. Just high school.

Q: Do you know where your family came from?

I know the town my father came from. Yeah, because when we were married fifty years, my daughter planned a trip and we went to Italy. Thank God. I have a bad back now. I can hardly walk. Yeah, Naples, a little town in Naples—Montella. We stayed there a couple nights. We went to the city hall. I understand very little of Italian. I could get by, but I cannot hold a real conversation. And we found out a lot of interesting things about my Dad. We found out that my father was told he was the oldest out of four children. He was born in Italy and I had two aunts and one uncle that was supposedly born in Philadelphia. Well, we found out my father had two older brothers. He was not the oldest, but he never knew.

(Shows interviewer some family photos) You want to see pictures of where my father was born? I will show you. Now my father and my uncles that lived in Philly and my aunt, they were always under the impression that my father was the oldest. But my father had two older brothers. I got the dates of when they were born and their names. At that time, maybe my grandmother could not afford to take three kids, so she only took the baby with her or maybe the other two died in transit and she ended up with one, which was my father. We will never know. This is my grandfather and this is my grandmother, Concetta Pizzi. And there is her family and there is (my grandfather's) family.

Q: Let us talk about your husband, Elmer, who grew up in the town of Elm (just outside of Hammonton).

His father was a stubborn Irishman. Never mind about school. You gotta go to work. They do not have nothing in Elm but a church and the little red schoolhouse that he used to go to. (He) quit in tenth grade. Both our kids were smart. Tommy was intelligent, but he always got in trouble.

Q: Did anyone take care of your kids while you were at work?

No, like I said, when they were babies, I was home. When I had Suzanne, I stayed home until she was in kindergarten. And that was it. When they were home, I would call them: "What are you doing?" "He is hitting me. He is hitting me." How could you go back to the sewing machine, when you hear all that crap? You had to. If you did not sit there and sew, you did not get paid. That was piecework.

(During the interview, Concetta's husband Elmer said she made $1.75 for every bundle of one hundred skirts that she made. On average, she turned out that many skirts in a half-hour.)

Q: Were you especially fast, compared to other people?

Yeah, but most of the sewing machine operators did piecework. I was a working wife. Today they are career women. And today, the career women go get takeout, whereas the working mother could not afford to get takeout and cooked all the time. My lunch hours were coming home (and cooking). Like if I knew we were having mashed potatoes, I would choke something down, stand at the sink, peel potatoes, and a lot of my friends said the same thing. Their lunch hour was not coming home for a half-hour watching television. It was doing something.

When I told you the last shop, by that time, my kids were both working. Well, Tommy might have been in college then. But my daughter, Suzanne, who is 53, she had two jobs that summer. She packed blueberries and she worked at McDonald's. We decided in Carousel Slacks, that we were going in a half-hour early and work a half-hour lunchtime. My half-hour lunchtime was picking her up at McDonald's, bringing her to pack blueberries. That did not last long. I said, "Look, this cannot work." I spent my half-hour on the road. She quit the blueberries because the McDonald's was year-round. Blueberries was seasonal.

Q: How do you spend your time these days?

We are not computer whizzes. I never wanted a computer. Then, about six years ago, my son-in-law said to me, "We are going to get you a computer." What am I going to do with a computer? He ordered it and that was the end. I know how to do e-mail (and) I know how to surf the 'net. That is all. I do not do nothing else on there.

But I always hear from my daughter and my son. My son more on the phone than I do from my daughter. Remember when I told you, I left Carousel Slacks and I spent a year down (in Atlantic City)? I really got educated down there. But like I said, it taught me how to work with money and when I came back I spent ten years at the bank. I only put a twenty-dollar bill in a penny machine but, in the summer, when the weather gets nice, my husband and I have a little walk because I cannot walk (very well). I have got spinal stenosis. We park at the casino and then we walk through. Then we sit on the boardwalk and watch the scenery, which is very interesting. It is like show and tell. Makes it very interesting.

Chapter 2

Sally Cappuccio-Pietrofitta

Interviewed by Blyss Bowman

The town of Hammonton, located in South Jersey, is a small town with a rich history. Many of the older adults that were born and raised in Hammonton are familiar with the garment industry that employed many women in the 1920s. Sally Cappuccio-Pietrofitta was the daughter of a garment worker named Grace Cappuccio, who was a hard-working seamstress in the factory for a number of years. Cappuccio-Pietrofitta was born in Camden in 1945. She grew up in Hammonton and lived there for her childhood and teenage years. She briefly lived in Pennsylvania while her husband was finishing college at Villanova University. Over the last forty years, she has lived in Linwood, Egg Harbor Township and Somers Point. For many years, Cappuccio-Pietrofitta has worked as the development director at the Missionaries of Sacred Heart in Linwood.

Growing up, she did not want to be a teacher or a nurse like most girls—she wanted to work in an office. Cappuccio-Pietrofitta did not have any aspiration to go to college but she took college prep courses and a business course in high school. She went to work at White Hall Laboratories right out of high school. She worked in different departments until she ended up in the accounting department. Cappuccio-Pietrofitta later got married and worked as a private secretary when her husband was in his last year of college. After her husband graduated college and became an engineer, she became a stay-at-home mom for sixteen years. She felt that she was very fortunate to be financially stable enough to care for her children in the home. This was an important value for Cappuccio-Pietrofitta and her husband. They agreed that Cappuccio-Pietrofitta would stay home with their children because they both grew up with mothers that worked in factories.

Cappuccio-Pietrofitta explained that her maiden name, Cappuccio, is of Sicilian origin. She stated that Cappuccio is a very common name in Sicily and would be comparable to the common surname of "Smith" in the United States. Both of her grandmothers came from the area around Naples and both of her grandfathers are from Sicily. Cappuccio-Pietrofitta's paternal grandfather was from the poor little town of Gesso in Sicily. She explained that many people in Hammonton are from Gesso. The original people that came over from Gesso discovered that the town of Hammonton was a good area for farming. These Sicilians then wrote back to their families in Gesso and encouraged them to come over in order to make money by farming.

Cappuccio-Pietrofitta stated that her maternal grandfather was a tailor and her maternal grandmother was a hand sewer. Her paternal grandfather was a common laborer who worked on the railroad and the farm while her paternal grandmother was a housewife. Cappuccio-Pietrofitta mentioned that on her mother's side, her mother was the first generation in her family to be born in the United States. On her father's side, her paternal great-grandfather had come to the United States initially and encouraged Cappuccio-Pietrofitta's grandfather to come to the town of Hammonton. Cappuccio-Pietrofitta stated that she does not speak Italian but her parents spoke it. Cappuccio-Pietrofitta explained that her parents spoke Italian among themselves when they got together with relatives at family gatherings.

Cappuccio-Pietrofitta's paternal grandparents lived in the (same) house and they did not speak English; they only spoke Italian and Sicilian or variations of both. Both Cappuccio-Pietrofitta's mother and father worked in the garment factory. Her father was a presser and her mother was a sewing machine operator. Cappuccio-Pietrofitta recalled that the very first time her parents met, they were working in a clothing factory that made ladies and girls coats. The shop was primarily female; however, the pressers were men. The workers made winter coats in the spring and summer and made the spring coats in the winter time; they did this so the coats would be ready for the seasons. Due to the "piece work" aspect of the factory, the workers wanted to keep working to make as much as they could.

Cappuccio-Pietrofitta explained that the work came in bundles. Her mother primarily worked on pockets, about thirty to fifty bundles a day. Each bundle of work had a ticket on it and the workers would write the number down in order to tell how much they did in the course of the day. Because of this, the workers felt pressure and incentive to keep working because the less they did, the less they made; there was no base wage per hour. Each worker had a book and kept track of her work.

Cappuccio-Pietrofitta described the rooms at the factory as being very big and open. The machines were side by side and up against one another; every worker had someone in front them. Cappuccio-Pietrofitta's mother's shop sat across the tracks from where Kramer Hall (on Front Street in Hammonton) is today. There were two big floors; the first floor was where the cutters worked. On this floor, there were long tables with materials and patterns. The fabric was stacked and large cutters would cut out the front piece of a garment, while another would cut out the sleeves. The fabric was placed in bundles and brought upstairs for the workers to start assembling them. Cappuccio-Pietrofitta assumed that the workers were set up in an assembly line. The back side of the building was where the big pressers (irons) were located. All of the pieces of fabric were pressed before the buttons were put on. The floor manager, along with some of the other men on the floor, would move the pieces along. They would make sure things kept moving and they would give the workers what they needed. Their role was to help to save time and maintain the flow of sewing. The last stop of the "assembly line" was a big table where someone would inspect the coats. At the end, the coats were shipped away. This assembly line pattern worked efficiently.

Cappuccio-Pietrofitta explained that it was not particularly common for children of the garment workers to go (visit their parents) at the factory. The children that went to the factory did not go nearly as much as Cappuccio-Pietrofitta and, when she was there, she was able to wander the factory. This is very different compared to today; due to the machinery, children would not be able to be present in such a workplace. Cappuccio-Pietrofitta stated that she spent a lot of time walking around and talking with the different workers; she described the workers as being very friendly.

Cappuccio-Pietrofitta's mother, Grace Cappuccio, worked on and off in the factory starting in the early 1920s; she would sometimes take time off when her children were born. Unfortunately, Cappuccio-Pietrofitta's father was diagnosed with cancer when she was two years old. Due to her father's illness and physical disability, it left him unable to work. Grace had no choice but to go to work to support the family. Cappuccio-Pietrofitta's father passed away when she was eight years old.

Cappuccio-Pietrofitta was the youngest of four; she had three brothers, two of which were already eighteen and older. Therefore, no one was home after school to watch her. Because of this, Cappuccio-Pietrofitta ended up walking about four or five blocks from school to the factory to wait for her mother until she got done work. Cappuccio-Pietrofitta would be dismissed from school around 3:00 p.m., and would wait with her mother until the end of her work day at 5 p.m. Cappuccio-Pietrofitta spent a lot of time in the garment factory.

Cappuccio-Pietrofitta explained that her mother often wished that she had the opportunity to be a nurse. Cappuccio thought she would have been good at being a nurse because she took care of a lot of people and was very hands on. She had the intelligence; unfortunately, she did not have the opportunity. Cappuccio-Pietrofitta's mother had to go to work right out of eighth grade, and did not go to high school. Her first job was at a shoe factory. She eventually became a very talented seamstress at the garment factory.

Cappuccio-Pietrofitta explained that some of her friends' mothers worked outside of the home but a lot were stay-at-home moms. She said it all depended on your financial level, the same as it is today. Once Cappuccio-Pietrofitta's father passed, her family only had her mother's income. Cappuccio-Pietrofitta explained that her mother's time was before the age of any type of entitlement society where you can get help if a spouse passes away. She said that there were very little options available back then. The only thing Cappuccio-Pietrofitta's mother got after her husband passed away was Social Security for her dependent children because they were minors. Cappuccio had a second job at Ideal as a sales lady part-time on Sundays and also sold Avon for a long time. At one point, she was supporting six people and herself.

Cappuccio-Pietrofitta was proud of her mother for being a very good seamstress. Cappuccio could make a whole coat which took a lot of talent and skill. Most of the women that worked in the factory only specialized in their particular area (i.e. sleeves, collars, buttons, etc.) and were unable to put together an entire coat. Cappuccio-Pietrofitta explained that when the different shops set out to obtain more work (i.e. a possible order of 400 coats), they would have samples made up of particular styles of coats with different patterns. They would then submit these samples to different companies. The companies, mainly around New York City and Philadelphia, would see if they liked the quality of the work. Cappuccio-Pietrofitta's mother provided these companies with many samples from the factory due to her impressive seamstress abilities. Cappuccio-Pietrofitta's mother even made dresses for her daughter and coats for all of her grandchildren.

Cappuccio-Pietrofitta and her brothers had chores they needed to complete around the house due to their mother working long hours. Although her father was physically impaired, he too would try to help out. Cappuccio-Pietrofitta's father would do the wash, make her mother's lunch, and would make the beds. The children set the table and dried the dishes. Housecleaning was on Saturdays. Cappuccio-Pietrofitta had three rooms that she was responsible for, her brother had two rooms and her mom completed the bathroom, kitchen and cooking. This was simply a responsibility the children had to complete and they "did not think twice about it."

In the summer, Cappuccio-Pietrofitta and her siblings worked picking blueberries. Cappuccio-Pietrofitta obtained working papers at the age of twelve and started packing blueberries. She would work until the end of July, seven days a week. There were no child labor laws about children working back then. Cappuccio-Pietrofitta would get picked up for work around 5:30 a.m. and would not get home until 6:00 p.m. The money Cappuccio-Pietrofitta made would buy her school clothes and prom gowns. Cappuccio-Pietrofitta stated that she was more aware back then about how hard parents had to work to have food on the table and keep the house going. Cappuccio-Pietrofitta stated that she appreciated things more and would not dare cause trouble because her parents "had it hard enough."

Cappuccio was eventually voted a chairlady by her coworkers at the garment factory. Being a chairlady, she was the representative that talked to the other union representatives on behalf of the people. Cappuccio-Pietrofitta admired her mother for this. Cappuccio-Pietrofitta admitted that it must not have been easy getting along with fifty women; however, her mother was able to mediate disputes and was therefore respected by the other women.

Cappuccio-Pietrofitta recalled that her mother never had time to do most of the things mothers could do with their children due to her work schedule. However, Cappuccio-Pietrofitta did not think too much about it as it was a reality of life; her mother had to work in order to support the family. Although her mother could not come to many extracurricular activities, Cappuccio-Pietrofitta did not feel abandoned as she stated that her mother was there "the rest of the time." Cappuccio-Pietrofitta explained that her mother had some time off in between seasons and this was "a treat." Cappuccio had vacation time during the first week of July and the family would go to the Steel Pier during that time. She also had off the day after Thanksgiving; they would go to Philadelphia and shop on this day.

After working at the garment factory for more than thirty-five years, Cappuccio retired around the age of 63. Cappuccio-Pietrofitta believes that her mother received health insurance through the factory as well as a small pension. Her pension from the union was $100 a month. When Cappuccio passed away in 1999, she received a death benefit of a couple of thousand dollars used for funeral expenses.

Cappuccio-Pietrofitta said that she thinks it must have been "mind numbing" for those workers to have to do the same piece of coat over and over. She believed that a lot of the women probably could have gone on to be teachers, nurses, and a lot of other things but many did not have the advantage to do so. Cappuccio-Pietrofitta wondered how they managed to do that type of work if they had a higher intellect or passion to do something different. She felt this may have led to emotional problems; these women may have wanted to use their brains or passion for something different but could not, due to lack of opportunity.

Cappuccio-Pietrofitta said that women have always gotten the "bum deal" and continue to do so today. She believes in equal pay and treatment among workers, regardless of gender. Cappuccio-Pietrofitta recalled going on a job interview in 1965 in Center City (Philadelphia) at an actuary firm. The firm was requesting a second-year male college student, as the actuary field is predominantly male. Although Cappuccio-Pietrofitta was not a male and was not in her second year of college, she had experience working in cost accounting. The firm wanted to hire Cappuccio-Pietrofitta, but refused to offer her as much money as a male student. They also inappropriately asked Cappuccio-Pietrofitta about her religion and if she was planning on having children. She was "annoyed" by this because it "did not seem right." Cappuccio-Pietrofitta did not take the job because she was offered a private secretary job instead. By taking the private secretary job, she did not have to pay the city wage tax or travel expenses. Cappuccio-Pietrofitta said she feels extremely lucky to have spent time at the garment factory and is very appreciative of how hard the women worked.

Chapter 3

Lucy Curcio

Interviewed by Stefani Pelly

Lucy Curcio was born on St. Lucy's Day, December 13, 1924, in Falling Waters, West Virginia. Her maiden name was Lucy Ezzi. Both of her parents were immigrants from Italy, who moved to West Virginia because many people from their native community had settled there.

Curcio moved many times during her childhood. Her family settled in West Virginia, and her father worked on the railroad there. The family lived in a railroad camp. Then, they moved to Philadelphia, back to West Virginia, then back to Philadelphia. During the late 1920s, her mother would take a bus to Hammonton to pick berries on the farms and then travel back to Philadelphia at night.

Curcio and her family settled in Hammonton in 1931. Lucy recalled being about seven years old and being at the farms while her mother picked strawberries, raspberries and blackberries. She said, "We tagged along, but you know as children, we were not very productive."

Curcio recalled that her mother had a very strong work ethic, just as everyone did back then. Her mother was widowed when Curcio was eight years old and she would work multiple jobs to keep her household afloat. In addition to working on the farms, she knitted clothes and did piecework in the garment factories. Curcio's father had passed away after being paralyzed by a stroke.

While her mother was picking berries at a farm during the early 1930s, she met another woman who said she could get her a job at the Kessler Clothing Factory making Hammonton Park Clothes. Subsequently, her mother started working at the factory doing piecework. Her mother would often bring bundles of work home at night to make extra money.

Curcio's mother worked at Kessler's Clothing Factory throughout the 1930s, and was a member of the union. She was one of many local women who worked outside the home: "We never gave it a thought (about her mother's job). Everybody worked. You know, when they came from Italy, nobody wrote any directions in Italian for them. They found jobs on the farm and in the factories. Everybody worked."

Curcio learned from her mother's work experience as a clothing factory worker: "As a worker, knowing that she knew what she had to do and she did it. She took very good care of us. She was a very good cook. She would take work home and hand knit. The faster you were, the more button holes you could make. She was very good at what she did."

At that time, every family had a garden and grew their own food. Curcio's mother made pasta from scratch, and they would preserve any food that could last through winter. In Hammonton, there were four whistles that went off daily; a whistle at 8:00 a.m. to start work, then a whistle at 12:00 p.m. for lunch, at 1:00 p.m. to return to work, and the last one at 5:00 p.m. to go home. Curcio said, "You always knew what time it was from the whistles!"

Unfortunately, her family fell on hard times and, one year, her mother did not have sufficient funds to pay for coal to heat their home. Her mother went to the welfare office but did not qualify since she had a job at the clothing factory. Mr. Kessler discovered that she could not pay for the coal so he reached in his pocket and handed her the money. He apparently knew all of his workers by name and was known for being a genuine and giving man.

Although she grew up during the Great Depression, Curcio was always grateful for what she had. She recalled, "None of us had anything to speak of. And no one was giving us anything either. There were no handouts like there are nowadays. But we did not even know we were supposed to be unhappy. My parents were good providers."

During Curcio's teen years, her first job was picking peaches on a farm. She also held a job at a furniture store in Hammonton making twelve dollars a week. After high school, she became a bookkeeper at a garment factory. It was during World War II. One day while she was at work, Samuel Curcio, a young man from Hammonton, came in to pick up his Eisenhower jacket. Curcio said, "And that's when it all started." Shortly after their first encounter, they started dating. Eventually, they married and started a family. They have been married for sixty-seven years.

Samuel Curcio was a lawyer who served in the state assembly while Frank Farley was senator. He played a large role in the creation of Stockton University in South Jersey.

In 1943, Curcio started working at the Newell garment factory in Vineland on the corner of Seventh and Quince Streets. At that time, many garment factories were making military jackets. After the war, the factory returned to making civilian clothing, including women's suits and jackets. Curcio often wore the clothing that was made there. She said that the mayor of Hammonton at that time was also the owner of the factory.

Curcio was a bookkeeper during a time when carbon paper was used to make copies, and all administrative work was done by hand. She would answer phones, make bids for product such as fabric, and make sure every employee received their share of money. She would take the company payroll to the bank accompanied by a police officer. Then, she would place the money in individual envelopes for each employee. Since there were many employees, Lucy had to stuff a lot of envelopes.

Curcio left the garment industry in 1949 because she and her husband started a family. She did not return to the workforce.

After she started working at the factory, her pay was raised to thirty dollars a week. She worked from 8:00 a.m. to 5:00 p.m. Monday through Friday. Since she did not have a car, she received a ride to work with men from her town. Few employees in the factory received an hourly wage, since it was mostly piecework. However, Lucy received a salary since she was a bookkeeper in the office and was paid by the week.

The managers of the factory, Mr. and Mrs. John Machise, were very respectful to their workers. Mr. Machise was the mayor of Hammonton during the 1940s. There were over 100 employees; both men and women worked in the factory. Women did mostly sewing while the men were the cutters, pressers and machine workers.

Curcio recalled, "It was amazing. The cutters would get the patterns. If one was cutting sleeves, he would stack the material so high and try to make the pattern perfect. The only cutters I have ever seen were men."

Curcio worked in the office that was attached to the factory. It was extremely noisy, so she would often close the office door when she used the telephone. In the factory: "There was no air conditioning. It was very hot. It was very noisy. There were so many rows of these noisy, noisy machines. It is amazing most of us can still hear. And the heat from all the pressing. The steam had no place to go."

When Curcio returned home from work, her day was not over. She and her sister had chores and they often helped their mother with the ironing. Her mother would do the laundry. Her brothers were in the service and away at war, so they were not home to do housework. Curcio would also help with cooking dinner, and cleaning up after dinner.

After graduating from Hammonton High School on a Wednesday in 1942, she started working a week later. The money that she made mostly went to her mother to support the household. She said this was common at the time. Curcio said, "For many years we did that. I had a sister that was three years older than me and she was dating and finally told my mother 'Look, I need to put my money aside' for what they call a 'hope chest' you know, buy linens, and whatever. After a while, I approached my mother the same way. I do not remember how we split it. Then, eventually I was the only one living at home."

According to Curcio, weddings during the 1940s often took place at home. Many years after she and Samuel married, her husband bought her a diamond engagement ring to go with her plain gold wedding band. It was something he had wanted to do for a long time but she always said no because she wanted to spend their money on the children.

If Curcio had any money left over, she would buy jewelry at a women's clothing shop called "Prince's," which was down the street from the factory. She still has some of the pieces. The wedding band that she still wears only cost sixteen dollars.

During her lunch break at the garment factory, she would eat lunch at a small restaurant that was connected to a drug store. At the restaurant, she was first introduced to cream cheese, and she liked it! This was a time when packaged and prepared foods were starting to be introduced to the general public. A loaf of bread cost ten cents, and milk was delivered to the doorstep.

Curcio, who earned thirty dollars a week at the garment factory, recognized the significance of the garment workers. She said, "Each individual was so important, it was their work, their skill. Every job was so important."

Chapter 4

Evelyn Kanjarski

Interviewed by Hok Yee Chau

Evelyn Kanjarski was born in Philadelphia in 1923. She was the oldest child in a family of fifteen siblings.

"My mother passed away when I was two years old. Then, my father remarried and had all the boys and girls. I only have one biological sister. I do have a big family indeed."

Her father was an electrician and her stepmother was a housewife who stayed at home and took care of all her children. Kanjarski grew up in a small town near Philadelphia. She said, "When I came to New Jersey, I was about seven or eight years old. When I was a little girl, I went to a Catholic school up in Philadelphia. But I grew up most of my life in Franklinville, the town where I am living now."

When Kanjarski grew up, she worked as a garment worker at Newell Clothing in Vineland. It was a "pretty big" sewing factory with a couple hundred employees. The factory was owned by Mr. John Machise, whom she described as wonderful and considerate. She recalled, "He was such a great boss, and I will never forget him. Mr. Machise would go to Vineland every day to make sure that the factory was kept clean and is being taken care of."

The factory was exactly nine miles away from home, so Kanjarski had to drive to work every day. She worked from eight in the morning to five in the afternoon every day. "Sometimes, we had to work on Saturday morning, so we could get the job done," she said. "But, we did not need to work overnight. That is for sure."

Her job there was to sew and make different kinds of clothes. When Kanjarski first started working at the factory, she made suits, coats and skirts: "But we were then forced to go on government work. We made army uniforms, navy uniforms and marine uniforms. It was a lot of hard work."

At nine o'clock every morning, Kanjarski and the other garment workers could have a fifteen-minute break to have a cup of coffee "but you brought that from home." During lunch time, workers had a half-hour to eat their lunch. Sometimes, she would bring in some soup and heat it on a pressure machine. "We were allowed to do that," she said with a smile. "We did not make a mess. It was like a second home there. You could do anything you want as long as you got it right. It's a good thing that we were not sloppy."

Besides eating in the factory, the workers had other options. Next to Newell Clothing, there was a restaurant called the New York Inn. The women sometimes went there to have their lunch, for which they paid. The only time the workers got anything free was during Christmastime.

After coming home from work every day, Kanjarski would prepare supper for her husband. They never had children. Besides going to work every day, she would go home and take care of the chores such as washing and ironing their clothes.

"When I first started my job, I did not make very much," she recalled. "If you made fifty cents an hour, you were lucky. The harder you worked, the more you made." The money she earned was used to pay for the electric bills, oil and food. "But I did save a little bit, and (sometimes) used it to buy something I liked."

Unlike other factories, not all the women at Newell Clothing were of Italian descent. They had workers who came from different backgrounds. Kanjarski once worked with a woman who was born in Europe. "We were all different," she said. "It was mixed, but the most important thing is that everybody got along." She remembered that there were a lot of workers from Puerto Rico when the factory was given up: "But, they were all nice and got along." She also recalled that the women in the factory were treated with respect by the owners.

"They had a really good crowd there," she said. "They were all good bosses. That was a wonderful place to work in. I never regretted it. Never."

The factory did have a union, called AFAL, and Kanjarski found it helpful for the workers. She said that after she retired: "I used to get a union pension every month. They gave a good pension and they provided good benefits. For example, if you got sick, you still got paid. If you had to go to the hospital, they paid for the bill. Yes, they took good care of you."

However, the factory only paid for a worker's benefit for a year if an employee retired. "Still, it was a good insurance," she said. When Kanjarski first started her job, the benefit was only nine dollars a month. But when she retired in 1982, it was almost one hundred dollars.

Kanjarski, who worked for the clothing factory for almost forty years, said that the best part of her job was the sewing because "always from a little girl, I loved to sew." Over the years, she has made a lot of clothes for other people. For herself, she not only made clothes but also the curtains in her house.

Newell Clothing closed in 1982, and Kanjarski has been retired ever since. The two factories left in Vineland are De Rossi and Crown Clothing. When asked whether she would ever have wanted to do something else for a living, she said, "Not really. Like I said, I just love to sew, and I still love to sew." She really enjoyed working in Newell Clothing, and she never regretted it: "Like I said, it was a wonderful shop to work in. Mr. Machise was the greatest, and I cannot say enough for him. I would say—he was one boss out of a million."

Now, Kanjarski lives in her own home, and enjoys every day of her life.

"I used to make about thirty to forty different kinds of cookies, such as prune and nut cookies, chocolate chip cookies, and sugar cookies," she said. "But I can no longer bake because of my health."

She enjoys watching her favorite comedies at home. Her niece, Melissa, helps her with the grocery shopping and schedules her doctor's appointments. "Melissa is such a sweet girl," Kanjarski said. "She really helps me a lot."

When asked what the most important thing she had learned from her past experience, Kanjarski replied, "Being a good friend, should not talking behind other people's back. If you cannot say anything good, then do not say anything. Also, be always thankful, and never take everything for granted."

Chapter 5

Susan Fognano

Interviewed by Janeen Wilson

Hammonton is located approximately twenty miles west of the beaches of Atlantic City and forty minutes away from Philadelphia. A number of garment factories once operated in the town, including one that was owned by Anna C. Bertino during the early twentieth century. The factory was located where Stockton University's Kramer Hall now stands.

Many of the garment workers at that time were Italian immigrants or the children of Italian immigrants. Hammonton native Susan Fognano grew up on Washington Street. She attended St. Joseph School from kindergarten through twelfth grade. She later married Rick Fognano, who went to her school's rival, Hammonton High School. Married thirty-five years, they have two children and two grandchildren of whom they are very proud. Fognano currently works at Hammonton High School.

She began working in 1975 in her senior year of high school as part of an internship program that was arranged with area businesses. The program allowed the students to go to school in the morning and work in the afternoon while receiving school credit. Fognano began work at the clothing factory as an intern doing payroll and was hired after graduation. She remained working there for more than ten years until the factory closed its doors.

Fognano got the job in the payroll department because they thought that she was good at numbers. As the youngest person in the building they made her feel at home, and she felt important to be learning to do payroll for one-hundred-and-fifty people. Her boss told her it was her job to know what everybody made because that was her job, but it was her job never to tell anybody else what she knew.

Fognano recalled that the factory workers were in the International Ladies Garment Workers Union (ILGWU) and made ladies coats and jackets. There were several shops in town and each specialized in something different. Fognano said: "Our delivery truck would come with large amounts of rolls of material; it would be unloaded on the elevator and went to the third floor. The cutters were on the third floor—the machines had a long blade of a saw which would cut the many patterns at one time. Everything got pinned with numbers and styles, sizes. From there it went on the elevator down to the second floor where the old fashion commercial sewing machines (were) with approximately a hundred workers. People were assigned to work on backs of coats, sleeves, making a pocket, inserting a pocket, sides, insert lining, making a hood, inserting the hood, making a belt, inserting a belt. Depending on how much time the job took there could be as many as six people doing the same job."

Fognano was amazed at how the workers would save time by tying a knot at the end of the thread with a different color and pulling it through the sewing needle. After they were finished, the coats went to the basement where people did "cleaning"—cutting off the threads and anything else that was hanging. From there, the garments would go to the presser and then be bagged for shipment in a big tractor trailer headed to New York.

It was a lot of work. However, everyone worked together and Fognano described everything as coming together like a big puzzle. The workers only knew their job; if they sewed buttons that is what they did, if they sewed pockets, that was all they did. So if someone was absent, the work sometimes had to wait until she returned. Very few workers knew how to do multiple jobs.

The workday started at eight in the morning and the workers took lunch from twelve to one, ending their day at five in the evening. They all punched (a time clock) in and out. If they lived close to the factory, some would go home for lunch. If not, they could choose to sit and eat at their machines. There was no smoking on the floor because it was too dangerous with all the material around: "The people who did smoke at times were not always at their machines which meant us, the office workers, would have to go out and find them and bring them back in."

For the office employees, the work day was not as long as that of the factory workers; they started eight thirty in the morning. Fognano said that everyone looked up to Bertino, the company owner. She was a good business woman who kept the factory clean; she had a night watchman who also cleaned every night before the workers came in the next day. Fognano considers herself lucky because she worked in the office where there was air conditioning but she did have to go into the shop a lot. The shop did not have air conditioning but it did have fans. The heat coming off the machines, especially the pressing machines, was horrendous and if the climate was very hot as well, Bertino would let the workers leave early. Fognano recalled, "The workers respected her and appreciated that she took them in, and they did not mind giving her a good day's work."

When asked about the cultural diversity, Fognano did not recall discrimination being an issue—both sexes and all nationalities were hired. The owner was willing to train people who did not have the skill they needed in order to give them a job. There were not as many men as females; the pressers and cutters were all men. There were a few men at the sewing machines. There were no gender issues such as sexual harassment or unfair pay wages mostly because the owner was a female. According to Fognano: "We had a lot of Italians, Spanish and Caucasians."

Fognano said, "I did not treat anybody any different or feel I that was better than anybody because I was an office worker." She recalled that when her son was almost one-year-old, he had on his pumpkin costume for Halloween and they wanted him to walk around the floor so everyone could see. The Italian tradition was to roll up money and place it in the child's hand and that is what the workers did for her son.

According to Fognano, Bertino was concerned about her workers and wanted to know if there were problems; she made them feel comfortable coming to her. There may have been little issues over material and some machine workers may have been envious of the floor workers because they got paid by the hour. When asked about advancement opportunities, Fognano said, "There was little room for advancement in the factory. Most people that worked there stayed until they retired or passed." To her, this was a great reflection of the work environment and the seeming satisfaction of the workers.

Vacation time did not accrue for the piece workers. The office workers received one-week of vacation for being there one year and two weeks for being there over ten years. Fognano accrued sick time and received medical benefits. Although the factory workers did not officially earn vacation or sick time, the factory would close for a week in July and this would be considered time that the workers could use as they pleased. If the workers were sick, the owner was very understanding and did not give them a hard time. It was a very family-oriented organization. The workers could get eyeglasses at Four Eyes in Voorhees for a minimal cost. The office workers received one week's pay as a bonus at Christmas time. The factory workers were offered a Christmas club and were given gifts from the bank at this time. The workers also received annual pay increases on their anniversary date.

Bertino would personally conduct evaluations with the workers reviewing their job performance for the year and informing them of their increase. The union was available to employees to represent those who felt that they were being underpaid or unfairly treated and to resolve any issues with their supervisor. Union dues were approximately six dollars per month.

The union offered the workers a pension fund with the ILGWU that they could collect when they retired. Unemployment was available if they were laid off. Twenty weeks of work and a certain amount of money had to be earned in order for workers to be able to collect unemployment, which was estimated to be about $130 at this time. In the event that someone retired before she was eligible to collect her pension, Bertino would sometimes allow that person to collect unemployment until she could receive her benefits.

"The Mount Carmel celebration was very big in our town and the factory would close for a half-day to allow the workers to attend the event with their families" recalled Fognano. Live bands would come into town and go around to different businesses playing for the workers. Bertino would allow the workers to stop and listen to the band and give the band a donation. Although Fognano did not grow up attending the procession, she often went once her half-day of work was finished. These days, it is a family tradition to participate in the celebration.

After work, Fognano went home and cooked dinner for her family, just like most of the other women. One luxury for the workers was to buy lottery tickets during their lunch break or after work. She said that some of them would spend ten to twenty dollars every day, which was a lot of money at that time.

When asked about the hardest part of her job, Fognano said when the office workers had a Monday off. When Fognano had a Monday off she only had one and half days to complete the payroll as opposed to the two and half days she would have when working on a Monday. The factory had a payroll company called Automatic Data Processing (ADP), one of the first payroll companies in the area. They came every Wednesday from Fort Washington to pick up the payroll and would deliver the checks on Thursday, which were then distributed on Friday. Her favorite part of the job: "I loved doing the bookkeeping part of the piece workers. I would do the bookkeeping part to add up the entries and make sure they balanced out. If the numbers were off, I had to go back to their books and figure where the mix-up occurred. I enjoyed the challenge of finding the problem especially when it resulted in owing the worker money."

One annual "perk" that she enjoyed was being able to get a new coat every year, a tradition that remains alive today. According to Fognano, she learned a lot from her former coworkers. She received numerous recipes that included zucchini lasagna, bread, and pizza. Her mother was German-Hungarian and her father was Italian so she did not grow up eating the seven fishes on Christmas Eve. However, she learned about the tradition from her coworkers.

Bertino's active interest in the community encouraged Fognano to help others as well. She believes that her former boss continues to have a positive impact on the community and local businesses in the area. She was also inspired by her coworkers: "They had much less than I have today and never complained; they did what they had to do." While most of the workers lived close, some came from other towns including Buena, Atco, Newtonville and Egg Harbor.

Finally, work at the factory began to get slower and slower until it came to the day that they informed the employees that they weren't going to open anymore. Fognano said, "When you look for the label and find that it was made in the United States, you may pay a little more but you are keeping someone here employed."

Chapter 6

Franca Fiori Gherardi

Interviewed by Lesya Popil

In Europe, you learn something; you always have something in your hands. When you come to a strange country, you feel a little bit lost, but then you use everything you know. My father made me a wood stick for a rolling pin and I used it to make pasta from scratch. You learn it there and you bring it here, you know? American youth should be taught home economics. They have to learn a trade; this is how I have so much work. You have to do it, that is it. From one job to the other, this is what America is good for. You can do anything you want to accomplish. We are here today, because we are blessed.

Franca Fiori Gherardi

Franca Fiori Gherardi was born in Lucca, in the province of Lucca, a city in the Tuscan region of northern Italy, on February 2, 1942. She went to school up until the fifth grade and then stopped because of the war. Gherardi has no pictures from her childhood. Her mother buried them for safety; however, they were destroyed during the war.

She grew up with four brothers and her parents, who taught her to work hard, be a proud woman, and to honor the family name. Growing up, her mother and father taught her to do daily chores. She helped prepare meals and take care of the other children in a busy household. At thirteen, her mother taught her to be a seamstress. Then Gherardi was trained by another teacher and went to a specialized school. While she lived in Italy, she worked in a factory that made men's shorts. During her three years there, she became engaged to Fred Gherardi, who filed an application for employment in America.

In September 1964, she married Fred. The following year, after waiting for two years for their application to be signed at the United States Embassy, they came to America. They signed a contract for one hundred dollars a week for Fred's work as a tailor. Before leaving, Gherardi recalled her father, Luigi, giving her a crucifix and saying, "Franca, no matter where you go, do not you ever forget." She has the crucifix in her house still today in her dresser drawer.

"I still think of this," she said. The couple said their goodbyes to their families and with two trunks between them, they sailed to America. They left in January on the LEONARDO DA VINCI. Gherardi said that it was very difficult to leave her family.

She did not realize how sad she was until the ship was leaving and she saw her family saying goodbye: "If it was today, I would never do that. When you are young, and they promise you things, you come to a strange country. It was not what you expected. Not at the beginning."

Gherardi said that the nine-day trip on the ship was terrifying for the couple. The waters were very rough. She said that she was not well the entire time and could not eat without becoming sick. She recalled, "They had a rope, if you had to walk across, you had to hang on the rope otherwise you will fall." They went to the top of the boat to get fresh air where no one was getting sick around them. The top of the boat was extremely cold.

She said that the bus ride following their arrival to America was also unsettling. She had a piece of paper with an address in her hand but she did not know where they were going and what would happen when they arrived in Hammonton. She remembered that it was snowing really hard.

When they arrived at the apartment in which they were to live, they were unhappy with the living conditions: "It looked like a witch house, really old, falling apart and so messy. You opened the lights, and tried to lay on the mattress, and the sides would fold up on you." They had no food and spoke only Italian.

That same evening, Gherardi met Dorothy Inferrera Orlandini's father, who offered her some warm soup. Although the Gherardis were afraid, Dorothy's family tried to support them. According to Gherardi, they never really adjusted to their living conditions but they "did what they had to do to survive." She said the people of Hammonton really helped her out: "They were good people."

When they were still in Italy, Fred had a tailor shop. He always worked in a suit and tie and his customers rarely saw him without his jacket on. Although the Gherardis were told that Fred would earn $100 a week for working as a tailor in the Kessler factory, they found out after they arrived that the factory would only pay $45 a week until they saw that he could work faster. Fred worked there for twelve years but had a very difficult time adjusting. In Italy, he was respected and worked very hard. When he got to the factory he was told to not wear suits any longer because, they said, ". . . only the supervisors wear ties."

Fortunately, he had a nice supervisor who encouraged him to not listen to any negative talk but he still suffered a lot of emotional and psychological stress. Gherardi had to push Fred to keep working because the working conditions were so terrible.

Gherardi began working at Kessler two weeks after Fred, in the pants department for $1.25 an hour. One month after she started work, she became pregnant. She was very frightened to tell the supervisor for fear of losing her job. Eventually a coworker told him and he spoke with her. She was very embarrassed, especially when he asked, "Is it true you are pregnant?" Although they told her that they could not give her full time work, she worked all nine months of her pregnancy, sometimes in 115 degree temperatures. In order to get some relief, she would put her feet under the sink because they would get very swollen.

She was becoming increasingly concerned about paying for the birth of her child. She was told to go to a clinic when she was going into labor and she would only have to pay $150. However, when she arrived, there were many women standing around the facility. Since she did not understand English, she did not feel that this was a safe environment to have her baby. She was four months pregnant with no doctor.

Eventually she found a doctor whom she told that she had no money. He said he would take care of her and she could give him the money when she had it. "He said, 'When you have it, you bring it to me.' He was wonderful." She paid a portion each month and eventually paid him off. When the baby was born, she named him after the doctor, Alexander Rodi.

Gherardi was often sad after the baby was born because she could not share him with her family. She wrote her family and received letters every two weeks. She recalled, "I received a letter from my mom and it had a little bib in the letter. It was really hard. I thought, 'Nobody is coming to see this baby.'" Four years later, Alexander was introduced to his family when the Gherardis visited Italy. She said, "Oh, that was amazing, there's nothing like it. But then leaving back again, that was tough."

When it was time for her to return to work, Gherardi was concerned about who would take care of Alexander. A woman offered to watch him every day while she worked. She recalled running home across a field at lunchtime to peek in the windows at her baby, returning to work with rosy cheeks from the cold.

She said: "I'd run back, and my foreman never knew." This went on for several years.

Eventually, after twelve years, Fred had to leave Kessler due to stress and for other health reasons after his doctor informed him that it was not healthy to continue working at the factory. Afterward, he struggled to get work because employers were concerned about his English. Eventually, he was employed as a tailor at Strawbridge's in Moorestown, a job that lasted twenty-four years. He dressed in a suit and a tie every day. He felt respected, did beautiful work and was very happy.

When Kessler opened another factory in Bridgeton, Gherardi was sent there to teach employees how to sew pants. She would go early in the morning and then come back and work in Hammonton. Kessler's business was failing and the company took fifteen percent out of their paychecks with the promise of getting eleven percent interest in return. Kessler closed in 1981 and they never received the money. Gherardi said, "A lot of people made a living with the company but we came at a different time. Conditions were different."

She continued to look for different ways to work. She worked several other jobs after Kessler closed. She sold Caesar ravioli and was paid $95 for three days. She taught Northern Italian cooking classes and adult education sewing classes at a program in Vineland. She also wrote a cookbook and, at forty, started her own sewing business out of her home. Gherardi said, "Sometimes I stop and think to myself, what a life you have to go through, but in a better way, though. But I always wanted to better myself."

Life for the Gherardis was challenging in many ways. However, they are very proud of their accomplishments, their family and of themselves. They are also very happy and proud to have lived an American dream.

Chapter 7

Anne Liberto

Interviewed by Dana Ciechanowski

Q: What is your name?
Anne Liberto.
Q: Where and when were you born?
I was born and raised in Hammonton.
Q: What jobs have you held?
I worked at the (sewing) factory from the time I was a teenager until it closed down. I was responsible for the job of anyone that called out. Mostly it was all on the bottom floor. I examined, I used to press the inner facings, did a few times the buttons, I never really actually used the machines on the second floor, I really did not do any of the machines.

Q: What do you do for a living now?
I am the Director of Membership Services for the General Building Contractors Association in Philadelphia.

Q: Do you know what country your family came from?
Italy in 1905.

Q: What do you remember about your town when you were growing up?
The (Feast of the Mt. Carmel) Festival every July; that everyone knew everyone. The community as a whole was very much like

family especially since they were a part of the Bertino family that ran the factory and provided jobs for much of the community.

Q: What was the name of the clothing factory you worked for?

The National Garment Company, located at 30 Front Street in Hammonton. It is now known as Kramer Hall. My family owned the factory.

Q: What did the company make?

Coats. All they made there was coats.

Q: Do you remember how big it was?

It was three floors. The entire building. My grandmother started the business in 1958 but she only leased the first floor. She built the business enough that she could buy the whole building. So each year she just kept getting bigger and bigger (and) by 1961 she had the whole building.

Q: How many people worked there?

At its peak they employed roughly 300 people; possibly almost 350. When production was slower they employed about 170-190.

Q: Where did you work?

I worked the shipping (and) receiving, basically quality control. Also, as I learned the different steps coming in, basically you name it, I did it.

David Liberto, Ann's father: "On weekends, on Saturdays, we cleaned the whole shop, what we called blow down all the motors. (We would) get all of the dust out of the motors, because when you are sewing and you are cutting materials and stuff, you get a lot of dust and it gets into your motors and all that and then every Saturday morning every motor got blown out so you did not have a fire or breakdown and such."

Q: Were all or most of the women of Italian descent?

David Liberto: "At the time that they worked there, the workers were all American citizens whose parents were most likely immigrants. Most of them were either of Italian or Hispanic descent but they were born here in the United States."

Q: What percentage of the workers was female?

David Liberto: "About eighty percent; mainly all of the sewers; only about two or three men did any sewing. The men were primarily in the cutting room and worked as pressers. There were about ten men in the cutting room and about ten pressers."

Q: Did everyone get along well?

David Liberto: "There was really a sense of, everyone's in this together."

Q: Was there a union?

They were unionized workers and they were also piece workers. They got paid per piece so, the faster you were on the machines, the more money you made.

Q: How many years did you work for the clothing factory?

David Liberto: "I started working there in 1965."

Anne Liberto recalled that she and her brother would come to the factory almost every day because their elementary school was right down the street so they would walk there when school let out. She described almost her whole family being there so it was great being able to go there: "We used to run all over this factory, I can still see David running around (with all of the female workers yelling) 'Oh, little David's here, little David's here!'"

Chapter 8

Gertrude Presti

Interviewed by Tatyana Duffy and narrated by

Her Daughter Joanna Conn

For every chapter in history there is a story, and this story is about my mother.

Gertrude Presti was born Conchete Spallone on October 31, 1914, in Philadelphia, Pennsylvania, to Antonio Spallone and Jennie Tartaglia Spallone. She was called Gertrude, and sometimes Gertie, because her mother preferred it over Conchete. Her father Antonio, according to Italian tradition, insisted she be named after a deceased relative. In the early 1900s some of Gertrude's relatives and in-laws migrated to America, never able to return to their homeland. They had to work in order to provide the "better life" that they initially hoped for upon relocation. Her maternal grandparents, known worldwide as the Colavita Olive Oil dynasty, were originally from Campobasso, Italy.

Not all immigrants were farmers, or masons, grocers or railroad workers. Some were tailors, and they contributed to the garment industry. Businessmen from established companies in America would send a contingent of their key employees to Italy to persuade these fine tailors to relocate to Hammonton. The fact that they would have employment, a home with better living conditions, schools and churches of their choosing and a better future for their next generation motivated them to come to America.

My parents spoke English, along with the maternal side of my family. My paternal grandparents spoke Italian and preferred to leave it that way. Their children learned and spoke both Italian and English. Stories about ancestors were at a minimum as both families were, for the most part, private people. I believe this came as a result of burdensome memories they didn't want to share. They were thankful they were able to come to America. They had housing, employment, a family, much better living conditions, so all of this was enough for them to overcome the nostalgia. It motivated them to provide a better future for the next generation.

Mom's mother, my maternal grandmother, was a homemaker; she managed the house and six children. My maternal grandfather worked on the railroad, and he along with his friends, made wine and sold it for extra income. My paternal grandmother was also a homemaker, who managed the house, eight children and worked on my grandfather's farm when time would allow.

Gertrude lived in Philadelphia until she was twenty years old. She left school early, possibly in the seventh or eighth grade, to help her parents by going to work. She worked in clothing factories in the city where she learned how to sew by OTJT or on the job training. During the summer months, when work was slow in the factories, she would travel to farms in South Jersey with family and friends to work in the fields. During a visit to a farm in Hammonton she met Anthony Presti and they began a pen pal relationship. Over a period of time, and with their parent's approval, they began dating. They married in 1934 and had two children, a daughter Joanna (me) in 1938, and a son Thomas in 1943.

Gertrude was a "garment worker" who specialized in "hand sewing." She was employed by the internationally known company

Hammonton Park Clothes, frequently referred to as Kessler's Shop. William B. Kessler, a Jewish immigrant from Austria, started the clothing business in Hammonton, New Jersey, in 1921. His original shop was on Front Street, then moved to Fairview Avenue, and finally to Tilton Street, where his dynasty took off! Kessler employed approximately 600 people. Mr. Kessler was always willing to employ people, part-time or full-time, not only to help them financially but to enhance his business as well. He was truly a reputable and kindhearted entrepreneur. His employees were "family" and over the years, those who retired continued to keep their friendship. My brother Tom worked at the shop after graduation from high school, thus the garment industry was his livelihood for a period of time, but then he moved on to the transportation field. Joanna's husband Robert was employed part-time as a salesman for DiPaola Clothes, where Hammonton Park Clothes was the largest part of their inventory. Again the garment industry came into play with the family, and many other families in town.

Garment workers had an impact on careers, because they were not only hard workers, but they were proud people and experts in their field. They were always clean and neat, they dressed in the best clothes they could afford, and were presentable at all times. The success of Kessler's encouraged other entrepreneurs into the clothing business. Therefore, several smaller firms settled in Hammonton and at times, employment was greater than 1,500 garment workers. The town was indeed the principal job outlet for the garment industry, and Hammonton Park Clothes was internationally recognized for making upscale men's suits along with sport jackets and slacks.

The shop was located behind our family home, perhaps 300 feet, more or less. Mom began working at the shop part-time after we started school. She was employed on a flexible schedule and as a result, my brother and I never realized she would go out to work each day. In the early morning she would help us prepare for school. Breakfast was served, sometimes lunch would be packed, and other times we came home for lunch since school was in close proximity to our home. When we arrived home for lunch, mom was there preparing our meal, and the three of us would eat together. We would go back to school, and she was out the back door to return to the shop. Sometimes, after school, I would go to the shop to see her, always having something very important to share with her. I remember her smile as I shouted out the details, and she never lifting her head, as she stitched the garment that indeed needed her undivided attention. I never felt neglected in any way as she divided herself among all her chores. There were times she would iron clothes late at night after everyone was in bed, or prepare dinner for the next day. There were also times when Mr. Kessler would send her home to complete a garment for a very important customer that had to be shipped out the next day. There she was, bent over carefully and skillfully sewing tiny, invisible stitches in a dimly lit area so as not to disturb any of us, regardless what we were doing. She was devoted to her craft as well as her family. My mother worked in the shop, tended to all duties that a wife, mother and homemaker did without ever complaining, while my dad worked two jobs, sometimes more.

My mother never tried to persuade me to follow in her foot-steps, but my father insisted I become a nurse, a career that I practiced for twenty years. My dream was to become a success-ful small business owner, so this was also accomplished. I was inspired by my uncle, who was a bookkeeper, and eventually owned his own business. I was not fond of sewing, probably because when I was in seventh grade, our sewing teacher (this was a required class) had us make a dress for a fashion show orga-nized by the Girl Scouts. Some of us struggled as we attempted to put a dress pattern together. It was exhausting and unpleasant, and she would hover over us making unpleasant sounds, as we tried to please her. Today, am I a seamstress? No! However, I can mend clothes with expertise. It's the apex of the triangle; garment industry, mom's genes and me.

I often think of our family, my ancestors, and their legacy. So many examples of survival. Doing what they knew best, sewing garments. It did not end there! My Aunt Kate would leave Kessler's Shop at 5 p.m. and hurry home to the farm never taking the time out to change her clothes. She would get on the tractor and plow fields in a dress. In later years, she had a business on Main Street, and would go there after leaving the shop. She would work until late in the evening. She set a fine example for me. My first job was delivering the local newspaper to the employees at Kessler's Shop. I worked on the farm, in retail, babysat; the list is endless.

My parents taught me to "give back." My father often volunteered for church activities, and my mother always found time for those in need. I became a community volunteer for various fundraisers. Mr. Kessler was well-known for his generosity to the community. He donated the largest sum of money to build a hospital. I was part of the group who secured funding for this much needed facility. In Mr. Kessler's honor, it was completed and dedicated in 1964 as The William B. Kessler Memorial Hospital, because he was indeed woven into fabric of Hammonton's history. His employees were "family" and over the years, those who retired continued to keep their friendship. My mother Gertrude was part of a closely knit group who would meet for lunch annually, at the same restaurant, same time, same conversations. Slowly they all passed, one by one, including my mom on February 13, 1998. It was obvious that Mr. Kessler, in his effort to expand the garment industry, kept people employed, productive and secure.

So here we are today, at least sixty years or more have passed. Gone, for the most part, are the days of custom-made clothes. Rituals are unheard of, and those times during the holidays, traditional spiritual celebrations, as well as family gatherings, are for some, gone by the way side. Certain customs and foods served on Easter, Yom Kippur, Thanksgiving, Hanukkah and Christmas seem to have lost their celebratory luster.

I recall after feasting on such an abundant amount of food, the adults would continue to sit around the table to chat and play cards. Children, who were to be seen and not heard, played with toys, listened to the radio, and loved to be outside if weather permitted. We were happy and content. Family was always our priority; this is what we were taught.

My dad continued to work, and work, and work. This is what he wanted, he made money for his family, he was productive and was loved by all. My brother spent as much time as possible on the farm. I can recall the quality time I spent with my mother. My mother would take me to the movies, the park and to the lake. We would visit friends, and they would talk for hours. Mom always attended our special activities, and was no doubt a big part of my life. When I was older, in my twenties, I would take her to New York to see a Broadway show, and go to special restaurants. Mom and I did so much together, I hardly know how to put it all into perspective. My mother and other women, especially those in the garment industry, set examples of empowerment through their fine skills, conscientiousness and earnings for what they valued. I was always reminded that "without the past, there is no future." My parents left me wonderful keepsakes, but the best was "the memory of them!"

Chapter 9

Mary Scarduzio

Interviewed by Brittany Mallinger

Mary Scarduzio was born and raised in Camden. She lived in a house with her mother, father, six siblings and grandmother. Scarduzio described the city as being "the most beautiful place." She explained that Camden got to be that way due to the hard work of the community: "Camden was so clean that you could have eaten off of the streets. That is how people kept their places. Every morning at 10:00 a.m., everybody came out and cleaned. They swept the sidewalks and scrubbed the steps."

As children, Scarduzio and her siblings had chores of their own. Her father would wake them up early on Saturday morning so that they would get to work. They were not allowed to sleep in on a weekend. The children would complain, as children are apt to do in the wee hours of a Saturday, but the work would always get done. Scarduzio's job was to scrub the family's large kitchen floor.

Her family had a philosophy: "You can have it, if you earn it. If not, you do not get it." So, the family earned their keep. Scarduzio said, "We had to work for everything we got. We had to do a chore, it was not handed to us." With the money that Scarduzio earned, she was able to enjoy her childhood. One of her favorite places to go was the five-and-dime on Kaighn Avenue for a hotdog and root beer. Also on Kaighn Avenue was a very popular ice cream parlor known as the Sugar Bowl. "On Friday and Saturday night, everybody would walk to the Sugar Bowl. Sometimes there were dances—they used to play the jukebox," she said.

Scarduzio started working in the garment industry at the age of thirteen. "I was thirteen, but I lied and said I was fifteen, because they would not hire you that young. My sister vouched for me." The first clothing factory that she worked for was Louis Seitchick, Inc. in Camden. Her sister had been working upstairs and heard that they needed a worker for the other floor, and so she brought Scarduzio to the factory for work. "Downstairs, they had collars for little fur coats," Scarduzio said. The collars were made of faux rabbit fur.

Prior to the women's Union of 1939, it was not unusual for Scarduzio to work forty-eight hours a week. She noted that she "still had to go to school, which they called 'continuation school.' It was not a regular school. You went to school one day a week, and then when you were sixteen, you did not have to go to school." A young garment worker, such as herself, could not just quit school. Therefore, Scarduzio went to school for one day a week, and upon turning sixteen, she no longer pursued her education and devoted her time to garment work.

At Louis Seitchick, Inc., Scarduzio started off working on the floor. She was what was known as a "floor girl." She said, "Floor girls were not pieceworkers. Floor girls were just girls who gave people their parts." Using a machine to sew, she and other floor girls would mark pockets and get the collars and fronts of jackets ready.

"We would fix the flaps and turn the belts. That is what I would have to do when I got there," Scarduzio said, "I had to turn belts. We made little girl's belts at that time."

Working as a floor girl could be demanding. They were under pressure by the pieceworkers to get the bundles ready. Scarduzio said, "If one girl was done and you did not have her bundle ready, then you would have to *move* because they would get irritated—because *they* worked on piecework." Every pieceworker had their own job. Scarduzio said, "Every girl was assigned a part. Whether it was a pocket, a collar, or sleeves. Every girl had one thing to do, and they did that continuously. But as a floor girl, you made one part of the coat and gave it to the next girl who would put on the sleeve, then gave it to the next girl who would put on the collar, and that was how it was put together."

The process of making a coat started off with the cutter: "The cutter would lay out the material, and it would go from one step to another." Scarduzio discussed the other methods involved in making the coats, such as the girls who worked on the lining and pressing process. "(The girls) made the lining just like we made parts of the coat. Another bunch of girls would put the lining on the coat, but in the meantime, all of the little pieces got taken to the pressers. They would press all the inside seams, so when the coat was almost complete and they did the finish pressing, they did not have to go in and press seams."

Scarduzio's boss was an operator who worked on the power machine. A girl who usually operated the power machine went away on her honeymoon for two weeks, and recognizing her interest, he asked Scarduzio if she wanted to give it a try. After she eagerly replied "yes," he then showed her how to handle the machine and told her not to go too fast.

"Those machines were very fast. You know how when you first start driving, you jerk the car around and it goes fast, and you learn to control (the speed)? It is the same with sewing," Scarduzio explained.

The other girl returned in two weeks, and then Scarduzio began making belts. Her usual pay was twelve to forty dollars a week during this time:

"When I started, I got two cents a seam. Do you know how many coats I had to do to make money at the end of the day? (The owner) would figure out how much to pay a seam so he could come up with a profit."

Trying to get pieces pressed was also stressful at times because a worker had to compete with other girls who had finished their pieces. "It was a free-for-all," Scarduzio said. "This girl began pressing hers first, and you had to wait until she was done pressing them." The pressers were an important part of the process. After the pieces were all put together, the pressers took over the finished product. They were in charge of tagging the coats and getting them ready to ship. The owner and designer decided on what would be the cost of the garment. Scarduzio said, "If we did not get (the sewing) done by a certain time, we would not get the money."

She worked at Louis Seitchick, Inc. making belts for a few years until Seitchick committed suicide. "That was the end of my job there," she said. "The whole place closed, and everybody was sent home. That was before the war. And then I did not have a job for a while."

After years of experience, Scarduzio got very fast at sewing. But even though she would sew quickly, she then would turn in just a certain amount of the pieces. She feared that if she turned in a lot of work, she would start being paid less per seam.

"If you are smart enough, you never went over a certain amount of money, as I did, because if you went over a certain amount of money they figured out she could do this faster, so she does not need that," she said. "We could take a cent a seam away from her—some days when you do not feel good or you do not work as fast, then you could (turn in the pieces). You had to use these tricks!"

There were some other tricks of the garment industry that Scarduzio got to know well. For instance, she recalled making the same coat for various companies. She said, "(The coats) would be shipped out to different stores. I knew they were shipping to Penny's, Lane Bryant. We would do the same coat, but in different colors for different stores so it would look like a different coat. Then we would put a Lane Bryant label in it, or a Penny's label in it." With a laugh, she said, "People who buy labels are out of their minds."

Scarduzio was out of a job for a period of time after Louis Seitchick, Inc. shut down. Then World War II began. With many men away at war, job opportunities opened up for women. She began working in jobs outside of the garment industry during the war. For a little while, Scarduzio worked at RCA. Interestingly enough, she also had a top-secret job stenciling boxes of rifles on 6th and Jefferson in Camden. She recalled, "I worked packing rifles. It was such a secret! It was for the government. Do not ask me what the name of the place was, I could not tell you. It was hush-hush!" Scarduzio said that nobody knew what was in the boxes because it was a government secret.

One of her brothers had a newsstand at Suburban Train Station located in Philadelphia on Filbert. He had men working for him at the newsstand, but the war took them away. Scarduzio was making more money stenciling than what a worker at the newsstand would usually make, but her brother offered to match her pay in exchange for her work. "So, I went to work with him until the boys came home," she explained. "And then I went back to sewing."

World War II came to an end, and in 1949, Scarduzio married her husband, Thomas. Then she began working for Modecraft, a clothing factory owned by Henry Pearl. Scarduzio went to the factory to apply, and after she told them how many years of experience that she had, she was hired and put right to work. "I did not even go home!" she exclaimed.

Scarduzio received about $180 dollars a week at Modecraft, which started out in Camden and eventually moved to Burlington. "We were in Camden for the longest time," she said. "The place got too small and then the trains went by it and interfered with the sewing machines."

The Burlington store was large, with a couple hundred workers who dubbed the factory "Burlington Coats." After Henry Pearl left the factory, the company evolved into what is known today Burlington Coat Factory.

While Scarduzio was working at Modecraft, she would buy some of the coats, taking advantage of her employee discount. She stayed at the factory until she became pregnant with her son, Thomas Jr. She noted, "I would have worked, but they would not give you your unemployment if you were pregnant. So, you camouflaged it and tried to work until you started to show, because once you started to show, they would not give (unemployment) to you." Scarduzio remained at home until both her son and daughter were in high school.

Scarduzio needed to go back to work to put her children through higher education. She recalled, "My son wanted to go to law school and my daughter wanted to go to college." At that time, her son was a junior and her daughter a freshman at Camden Catholic High School. Her family was not able to receive financial aid, due to her husband having a job as a sheet metal worker.

"It was a good job for that time, but it was not enough to put two kids through college," Scarduzio said. "So, I went back to work."

One day, Scarduzio happened upon an interesting advertisement while reading the paper. It read: "OPERATOR WANTED. POWER MACHINE. WE WILL TEACH." Scarduzio had never seen an advertisement like that in her life. Slightly bewildered, she told her husband, Thomas, about it: "That was crazy. I did not know who would put a thing like that in there. They did not teach you; you learned (from another worker)."

Scarduzio answered the advertisement because the company was located close to home on Cuthbert Boulevard in Camden. A man asked her if she knew how to run the machine and how many years of experience she had. Scarduzio let him know that she had about thirty-five years of experience up until that point. When he heard her response, he left the room for a long while, leaving her in suspense. She still had no idea what the company was even going to produce.

Eventually the man came back with another man who talked for a long time, and then told her that she was hired.

"What am I hired for?" Scarduzio asked, still not knowing what the company made. The men told her that they sold parachutes. She exclaimed, "I never sewed a parachute!" But the men told her that if she had sewed for thirty-five years, she could sew a parachute. Two weeks later, Scarduzio officially began making parachutes for Paraflight in Camden County, and she loved working for them.

The person who taught her how to put the parachutes together was a very nice man from Hungary. She found it easy to do the work once she had been instructed what to do.

"So, I whizzed through one panel," Scarduzio said. The man was astonished and remarked how quickly she sewed. She answered, "That was not fast. That was just what I do." Both the man from Hungary and another man who was from Texas laughed at Scarduzio's response. The man from Texas said that they had been trying to make the parachute on a treadle machine, which Scarduzio saw as being a novice move. "You can tell they never sewed!" she said with a laugh.

Scarduzio became a floor lady at Paraflight.

"I was the 'Big Wheel,'" she said proudly. "I showed everybody else what to sew."

Scarduzio was given the responsibility of hiring workers. She recalled, "I had a nice crew of ladies. They worked there and all had their own little operation to do." Paraflight was the best company for which Scarduzio had ever worked: "Henry Pearl was an ace, but (Paraflight) gave me six paid sick days a year," as well as a week's vacation within the first few months of her employment. Never in all of her life had she been given vacation after less than a year of working or gotten paid for a sick day. She worked there until her husband passed away, and retired in 1984. She was sixty by then.

After Scarduzio finished making the first parachute, they drove out to an airport in Medford to test it, which made her very nervous. However, the men knew that the parachute would work. Scarduzio learned about the process that parachutes go through to ensure the safety of jumpers. "What they do after we sew it is, it goes through another operation, and they put it on a light table, and they pull a sheet over it," explained Scarduzio. "There was a girl who examined the seams to see if there was a stitch missing. If there is, that 'chute did not go up, because it would get air in it and explode." Nonetheless, Scarduzio reported being scared to death.

The jumpers who tested out the parachutes were three young men who loved to fly. Scarduzio recalled: "When they went up, I could not wait for them to come down." Once the boys made it back down safely, they gave Scarduzio a big hug, knowing that she was so frightened for them.

Paraflight repaired many parachutes for the military. According to Scarduzio, "The Army guys brought (the parachutes) in, and (Paraflight) fixed them." The men of Paraflight continued being kind to her following her retirement. She said, "When my husband died, I had never collected any of my sick days. Did you know they gave me all of my sick days from when I was there? They brought me a check every week. That was my last sewing for a while until I went to live with my daughter."

Scarduzio and her late husband, Thomas, made quite a team. They worked together to create beautiful dresses. Thomas had a degree in designing sheet metal, and he used his skill to draw dresses for his wife. Scarduzio then looked at the drawings and sewed dresses for herself. Although it has been over thirty years since his passing, it is easy to gain a sense of the camaraderie and love that the couple has been able to share for one another. Thinking back on her relationship with her husband, Scarduzio said, "I was fortunate, let us put it that way. I had a great husband, and my children talk about him every day."

After Thomas died, Scarduzio stopped working and went to live with her daughter and grandchildren. When her three grandchildren were in school, she went back to work. For two years, Scarduzio sewed for a company in Hammonton known as Modern Clothing. She explained, "I went to Hammonton for a couple of years. That was it. By that time, I was in my seventies."

She noted that most of the women of Hammonton were of Italian decent, like herself. Ultimately, the closing of the factories led her to officially retire. Scarduzio said, "If I could get a job today, I would go to work. But there are no sewing places around. They have done away with them. Everything is overseas. So that is why I ain't working."

Scarduzio recalled while she was still working, the union made it possible for the employees to only work a maximum forty hours a week. However, she does not recall much good coming from the Union for her personal betterment. "In the ladies garment (business), they started the Union in 1939," she said. Union members had to pay two dollars a month in dues.

By cutting the workers' hours, Scarduzio and some of her coworkers received smaller paychecks. The women working piecework were forced to generate more sewing in order to maintain their wages. Meanwhile, everyone had to pay the same Union dues, which was easier for a pieceworker than a floor girl.

And while the Union collected dues for many years, Scarduzio said, "It was many years before they were ever able to give you anything." Moreover, when she returned to garment work after having her children, she had to return as a new Union member despite having paid her dues for years. She also found that sexism led men to get paid better than the women.

Scarduzio found that she never got a full week's pay as a garment worker for the Union: "You made a percentage of what you made. You never knew what you were going to get." Furthermore, nobody was given compensation. In the event of a work-related emergency, the workers were taken to the hospital, and that was all.

Interestingly enough, Scarduzio never wanted to do anything else for a living. She really enjoyed sewing. While others might have only sewed for the paycheck, Scarduzio sewed all of the time. Her daughter, Maria, never had to purchase a coat until high school. Scarduzio also never bothered buying dresses for herself or clothing for her children when they were small.

Now in her nineties, Scarduzio continues to sew for the love of it. She said that sewing keeps her busy, and she will not turn down requests from her family members to sew for them. "I sew at home," she said. "I sew for my family and do not get paid. Everything I have done, I have done as charity. They wanted it, I did it."

However, like other women of her generation, Scarduzio was sometimes forced to miss out on opportunities because there was no money to pay for such things:

"I wanted to go for (lessons). You went to school and they taught you sewing and designing. That course was $500. I did not have no $500, and it was not part of the college curriculum— just sewing. A lady friend asked me to go with her, and I said I cannot afford it. (When) my older brother was married, he said to me, 'Babe, I will give it to you, and you can pay me back.' I said, 'I cannot do that! How am I ever going to pay you back? I only make twelve dollars a week, and I need to give Mom eleven!' He started laughing and said, 'No, you can take your time and give it back to me.' That is the one thing I really regret I did not do. I could have gone there, and maybe, who knows, I could have had my own business. That other girl did. She had her own business—sold wedding gowns, draperies, and everything. That was my one mistake."

For the last thirty years, Scarduzio has been living with her daughter and son-in-law in Shamong. One of her grandchildren is an engineer at Cornell University in New York while the other two children are involved in computers. Scarduzio's son, Thomas Jr., lives in Arizona and serves as a judge. One of his daughters is a professor of Communications, while the other is head coach of a sand volleyball team at Arizona State University. Scarduzio is the great-grandmother of three children and is very proud of her family.

Epilogue

Including an Oral History assignment in a graduate-level course on *Aging: Advanced Practice* was one of the best "teaching moments" a professor can have. To introduce young students majoring in social work to the realities of aging immigrant women in the workplace, and have them experience magical moments of interview interactions and editing epiphanies about the importance of unions, workplace policy, family values and economics was pure fun. Through these interviews bonds were formed, relationships were built, and historical information was garnered and now archived for future generations.

With gratitude, we thank the students who spent many hours traveling, interviewing, recording, editing and polishing final word documents of dialogue—stories about the garment industry. Vineland historian Patricia A. Martinelli deserves thanks for her commitment to the project, editing of early student drafts and finalized publishable copy. To the Stockton Center on Successful Aging, the South Jersey Culture & History Center, the staff of Kramer Hall, and Stockton University's MSW Program we give credit for the sponsorship and support in completing this project and archiving this information.

Colophon

Interviews for this volume were completed by BS in Social Work major Hok (Zora) Chau and the following graduate students who were enrolled in Dr. Lisa Cox's spring 2015 semester SOWK 5530, *Aging: Advanced Practice* class: Blyss Bowman, Dana Ciechanowski, Tatyana Duffy, Barbara Edelhauser, Brittany Mallinger, Stefanie Pelly, Lesya Popil, and Janeen Wilson. Lisa Cox, Patricia Martinelli and Christina Birchler served as editors for this volume. Kristina Boyer completed final copy editing, typesetting and book design. Heidi Hartley designed the cover and Tom Kinsella supervised the publication.

CPSIA information can be obtained at www.ICGtesting.com
Printed in the USA
BVOW08s0759040716

454345BV00002B/389/P